My Notes

...True friends are never apart, maybe in distance but never in heart....

My Notes

My Notes

...True friends are never apart, maybe in distance but never in heart....

My Notes

My Notes

...True friends are never apart, maybe in distance but never in heart....

My Notes

My Notes

...True friends are never apart, maybe in distance but never in heart....

My Notes

My Notes

...True friends are never apart, maybe in distance but never in heart....

My Notes

My Notes

...True friends are never apart, maybe in distance but never in heart....

My Notes

My Notes

...True friends are never apart, maybe in distance but never in heart....

My Notes

My Notes

...True friends are never apart, maybe in distance but never in heart....

My Notes

My Notes

...True friends are never apart, maybe in distance but never in heart....

My Notes

My Notes

...True friends are never apart, maybe in distance but never in heart.....

My Notes

My Notes

...True friends are never apart, maybe in distance but never in heart....

My Notes

My Notes

...True friends are never apart, maybe in distance but never in heart....

My Notes

My Notes

...True friends are never apart, maybe in distance but never in heart....

My Notes

My Notes

...True friends are never apart, maybe in distance but never in heart....

My Notes

My Notes

...True friends are never apart, maybe in distance but never in heart....

My Notes

My Notes

...True friends are never apart, maybe in distance but never in heart....

My Notes

My Notes

...True friends are never apart, maybe in distance but never in heart....

My Notes

My Notes

...True friends are never apart, maybe in distance but never in heart.....

My Notes

My Notes

...True friends are never apart, maybe in distance but never in heart....

My Notes

My Notes

...True friends are never apart, maybe in distance but never in heart....

My Notes

My Notes

...True friends are never apart, maybe in distance but never in heart....

My Notes

My Notes

...*True friends are never apart, maybe in distance but never in heart...*

My Notes

My Notes

...True friends are never apart, maybe in distance but never in heart....

My Notes

My Notes

...True friends are never apart, maybe in distance but never in heart....

My Notes

My Notes

...True friends are never apart, maybe in distance but never in heart....

My Notes

My Notes

...True friends are never apart, maybe in distance but never in heart....

My Notes

My Notes

...True friends are never apart, maybe in distance but never in heart....

My Notes

My Notes

...True friends are never apart, maybe in distance but never in heart....

My Notes

My Notes

...True friends are never apart, maybe in distance but never in heart....

My Notes

My Notes

...True friends are never apart, maybe in distance but never in heart....

My Notes

My Notes

...True friends are never apart, maybe in distance but never in heart....

My Notes

My Notes

...True friends are never apart, maybe in distance but never in heart....

My Notes

My Notes

...True friends are never apart, maybe in distance but never in heart....

My Notes

My Notes

...True friends are never apart, maybe in distance but never in heart....

My Notes

My Notes

...True friends are never apart, maybe in distance but never in heart....

My Notes

My Notes

...True friends are never apart, maybe in distance but never in heart....

My Notes

My Notes

...True friends are never apart, maybe in distance but never in heart....

My Notes

My Notes

...True friends are never apart, maybe in distance but never in heart....

My Notes

My Notes

...True friends are never apart, maybe in distance but never in heart....

My Notes

My Notes

...True friends are never apart, maybe in distance but never in heart....

My Notes

My Notes

...True friends are never apart, maybe in distance but never in heart....

My Notes

My Notes

...True friends are never apart, maybe in distance but never in heart...

My Notes

My Notes

...True friends are never apart, maybe in distance but never in heart....

My Notes

My Notes

...True friends are never apart, maybe in distance but never in heart....

My Notes

My Notes

...True friends are never apart, maybe in distance but never in heart...

My Notes

My Notes

...True friends are never apart, maybe in distance but never in heart...

My Notes

My Notes

...True friends are never apart, maybe in distance but never in heart....

My Notes

My Notes

...True friends are never apart, maybe in distance but never in heart....

My Notes

My Notes

...True friends are never apart, maybe in distance but never in heart....

My Notes

My Notes

...True friends are never apart, maybe in distance but never in heart....

My Notes

My Notes

...True friends are never apart, maybe in distance but never in heart....

My Notes

My Notes

...True friends are never apart, maybe in distance but never in heart....

My Notes

My Notes

...True friends are never apart, maybe in distance but never in heart....

My Notes

My Notes

...True friends are never apart, maybe in distance but never in heart....

My Notes

My Notes

...True friends are never apart, maybe in distance but never in heart.....

My Notes

My Notes

...True friends are never apart, maybe in distance but never in heart....

My Notes

My Notes

...True friends are never apart, maybe in distance but never in heart....

My Notes

My Notes

...True friends are never apart, maybe in distance but never in heart....

My Notes

My Notes

...True friends are never apart, maybe in distance but never in heart....

My Notes